Diet recommendations during TCM - Liver - Wind with Yang Rising

Please check these recommendations always with a nutrition consultant, therapist, doctor or dietician. The recipes and the list of ingredients are supporting the conventional medical therapy. The calorie disclosures of fresh ingredients (fruit and vegetables) vary according to quality and time of harvest. The contents were checked by a dietician and a nutrition consultant for the Traditional Chinese Medicine (TCM).

Author:
©2020 Josef Miligui
www.ebns.at

AF176713

Source:
The lists are created from the EBNS database for nutritional counseling. The database is used by dietitians, therapists and doctors for advising the patient / client.

Literature:
The specialist literature and the training documents of the German and Austrian dietary and traditional Chinese medicine serve as a knowledge base. We have used the documents as a basis of knowledge, adapted it to our experience and completed them.
http://nutribook.info/

Production and publishing:
BoD – Books on Demand, Norderstedt
ISBN: 9783752856996

Diet recommendations for TCM - Liver - Wind with Yang Rising

1   Treatment strategy

Drink 3 cups of tea blends daily. After 6 weeks, check if the syndromes are still here. If you are taking any medication, please discuss the interactions with your doctor.

2   Avoid

n.a.

3 Recipes

(rec.) = You can use more.
(little) = You should use less than specified
(omit) = omit.

3.1 Celery and tomato salad

Nourishes liver-Yin, produces humors, brings the liver Qi in motion,
cools heat, relaxes, builds up Qi.
Cooking time approx. 10 min
Calories p. portion: 245
1 portions
Allergens: GHL

Quantity of ingredients
Celery sticks 3-4 twigs / 50g. (rec.) - cool - sweet....................................earth
Tomato 4 pieces / 200g. (yes) - cold - sweet-sour ....wood
Basil 3 leaves (fresh) / 1g. (rec.) - warm - acrid, bitter .... fire
Basil 3 leaves (fresh) / 1g. (rec.) - warm - acrid, bitter .... fire
Yogurt (natural, 1.5% fat) 3 table spoons / 30g. (rec.) - cool - sour ....wood
Olive oil 1/2 teaspoon / 5g. (yes) - cool - sweet ....earth
Lemon juice 1 table spoon / 10g. (rec.) - cold - sour ....wood
Salt 1 pinch / 0,5g. (little) - cold - salty .... water
Sugar white 1 pinch / 0,5g. (little) - cold - sweet....................................earth
Pepper (ground) 1 pinch / 0,2g. () - warm - acrid ....metal
Hazelnuts 2 table spoons / 20g. (yes) - neutral - sweet ....earth

Cooking instructions:
Clean celery, possibly remove threads and cut into fine rings. Wash
tomatoes and dice. For the sauce, mix yoghurt with olive oil and lemon
juice and season with the spices. Add the prepared tomatoes and
celery to the sauce and mix. Finely chop whole hazelnuts or sprinkle
ground hazelnuts over the fresh food and serve the salad garnished
with basil leaves.

3.2 Cooling rice dish with grapefruit

Lowers lung Qi, nourishes fluids, dissolves mucus, dries out, passes downwardly, warms the stomach and spleen, harmonizes the intestine, forces Qi, reduces moisture, strengthens Qi and Kidney Jing, moisturizes, relaxes, builds up Qi, spreads.
Cooking time approx. 20 min
Calories p. portion: 234
4 portions
Allergens: GHO

Quantity of ingredients
Rice round grain 1 cup / 120g. (rec.) - neutral - sweet .... metal
Water 5 cups / 600g. (yes) - cool - salty .... earth
Hazelnuts 2 table spoons / 20g. (yes) - neutral - sweet .... earth
Raisins 2 table spoons / 20g. (little) - warm - sweet .... earth
Agave nectar 1 table spoon / 10g. () - cool - sweet ....*
Salt 1 pinch / 0,2g. (little) - cold - salty .... water
Almond puree 1 table spoon / 10g. (little) - neutral - sweet .... earth
Grapefruit (Pomelo) 1 piece / 200g. (yes) - cool - sweet, sour .... fire
Butter organic 2 teaspoons / 20g. (yes) - neutral - sweet .... earth

Cooking instructions:
Preparation on the eve: Pour round grain rice into cold water and cook. Soak chopped hazelnuts and raisins in some hot water overnight.

In the morning: Stir in a little hot water some agave syrup; add the rice and heat; add a small pinch of salt, almond paste, chopped grapefruit, the soaked chopped hazelnuts and raisins and mix; Serve with a small piece of butter.

3.3 Tea from celery sticks

Brings the Liver Qi in motion, cools heat, moisturizes, relaxes, builds up Qi, spreads.
Cooking time approx. 15 min
Calories p. portion: 1
4 portions
Allergens: L

Quantity of ingredients
Celery sticks 2 table spoons (chopped) / 18g. (rec.) - cool - sweet .... earth
Water 2 cup / 500g. (yes) - cool - salty .... earth

Cooking instructions:
Heat the water till it boils and put it aside. Add cutted celery and cook for 10 min. to let go. Strain. Sweet to taste with honey.

3.4 Tea from chamomile

Reduces internal wind and heat, cools liver.
Cooking time approx. 10 min
Calories p. portion: 0
1 portions

Quantity of ingredients
Chamomile 1 teaspoon / 3g. (rec.) - cool - sweet, bitter.................................*
Water 1 cup / 120g. (yes) - cool - salty..earth

Cooking instructions:
Heat the water till it boils and put it aside. Chamomile flowers added and 10 min. to let go.

3.5 Tea from sage

Distributes mucus, passes downwardly, activates Wei Qi, forces Qi.
Cooking time approx. 15 min
Calories p. portion: 4
4 portions

Quantity of ingredients
Sage 2 teaspoons / 6g. (rec.) - neutral - bitter, spicy ....fire
Water 2 cup / 500g. (yes) - cool - salty..earth

Cooking instructions:
Heat the water till it boils and put it aside. Add sage and 10 min. to let go. Strain. Sweet to taste with honey.

3.6 Tea from yarrow

Dries out, passes downwardly.
Cooking time approx. 15 min
Calories p. portion: 0
2 portions

Quantity of ingredients
Yarrow tea 2-4 teaspoons / 6g. (rec.) - cold - bitter ....fire
Water 2 cup / 500g. (yes) - cool - salty..earth

Cooking instructions:
Heat the water till it boils and put it aside. Add yarrow and 10 min. to let go. Strain. Sweet to taste with honey.

3.7   Tea mixture TCM - Liver - Rising Liver Yang

Acts against rising liver-yang, clears moisture-heat in the liver.
Cooking time approx. 15min.
Calories p. portion: 0
2 portions

Quantity of ingredients
Yarrow 5g. / 5g. () - cold - bitter...*
Dandelionroots tea 5g. / 5g. (rec.) - cold - bitter ....*
Balm 7g. / 7g. (yes) - warm - bitter ....wood

4   Effects of food

4.1   Use ingredients: recommendable

Agar agar (kelp)
Barley
Barley not peeled
Basil
Burdock root tea
Celery root
Celery sticks
Chamomile
Chickpeas
Coconut meat
Dandelionroots tea
Green tea
Lemon
Lemon juice
Lime
Mulberry fruit
Mung bean sprouting
Mussels
Orange
Quinoa
Rabbit liver
Rhubarb
Rice (fragrance)
Rice (whole grain)

Rice Basmati
Rice black
Rice flour
Rice long grain rice
Rice red
Rice round grain
Rice sweet
Rice variety any
Rice wild (nature rice)
Sage
Salsify
Seacrab
Sesame, black
Sorrel
Soybeans, black
Soybeans, yellow
Tsampa (roasted barley flour)
Yarrow tea
Yogurt (natural, 1.5% fat)
Yogurt (natural, 3.5% fat)

4.2   Use ingredients: yes

Adzuki beans
Amaranth
Apple (sour)
Apple (sweet)
Arrowroot
Artichoke
Asparagus (green or white)
Aubergine
Avocado
Balm
Bamboo shoots
Banana
Banana (cooking banana)
Basic recipe for a rice soup (Congee)
Beef liver
Beer (Pils)
Beer (Top-fermented German dark beer)
Blackberry´s
Black-eyed peas
Blueberry
Blueberry juice
Boletus mushroom
Breadcrumbs (wheat bread, bread roll)
Broad beans (thick beans)
Broccoli
Brussels sprouts
Buckwheat
Bulgur (cereals)
Butter organic
Buttermilk
Calamari
Cantaloupe
Carambola (Star fruit)
Carp
Cashews
Cauliflower
Caviar
Champignon
Chanterelle
Chard
Chicken stomach
Chicory
Chinese cabbage
Chlorella (fresh water)
Clementines
Coconut flakes
Coconut grated
Cod
Coix (seeds) YiYi Ren
Couscous

Cow's milk (1.5% fat)
Cow's milk (whole milk 3.5% fat)
Crab
Cranberry
Cranberry juice
Cress
Crucian
Cucumber
Curcuma
Currant (black)
Currant (red)
Currant (white)
Dandelion (young plants)
Duck (heart)
Duck (slaughtered)
Elderberry blossom tee
Endive salad
Fig
Fig dried
Fish pieces mixed (fresh water)
Fresh cheese
Goose
Goose parts
Gooseberry
Gourd
Grape juice red
Grape juice white
Grapefruit (Pomelo)
Grapefruit juice
Grapes red
Grapes white
Ground
Ground caraway
Hazelnuts
Herbs various
Herring
Honey
Iceberg lettuce
Kiwi
Kombu seaweed (Saccharina japonica)
Lamb's lettuce
Lamb's lettuce
Lemon peel
Lentils
Lentils black
Lentils red
Lentils yellow
Lettuce
Lobster
Lychee
Lychee in Preserved

Mallow (Malva sylvestris) blossom tea
Malt
Mango
Maple syrup
Margarine
Margarine (diet)
Millet
Millet flakes
Miso paste (soy bean paste)
Morel (black, dried)
Morel, dried
Mozzarella
Mullet
Mung bean
Octopus
Olive oil
Olives
Oysters
Parmesan
Parsnip
Peanut oil
Peanuts
Pear
Pear juice
Peas
Peas, green
Perch
Pigeon
Pine nuts
Pineapple
Pineapple juice without sugar
Pistachios
Plaice
Plum
Pork liver
Potato
Pumpkin seeds
Quince
Rabbit
Rabbit meat
Radicchio
Radish
Radish black
Rapeseed oil
Raspberry
Raspberry dried (immature)
Red beet
Red cabbage
Reishi mushroom
Rice malt
Rice noodles
Romaine lettuce / lettuce salad
Rye

Rye flour
Saffron
Salmon
Sauerkraut (cutted cabbage fermented)
Sesame oil
Sesame paste (Tahini)
Shark
Shiitake, dried
Shrimp
Sour cherries
Soy flour
Soy sauce
Soy Tofu
Soya Cuisine (soy cream)
Soybean milk
Soybeans
Spelled (Dark) bread
Spelled grain
Spelled semolina
Spelled wholemeal flour
Spinach
Strawberries
Strawberry Juice
Sugar cane sugar
Sugar fructose - fruit sugar
Sugar glucose - grapes sugar
Sugar Milk Sugar
Sunflower oil
Sunflower seeds
Tangerine
Tarragon (Estragon)
Tomato
Trout
Tuna
Vanilla
Vanilla powder
Vegetable juice
Wakame
Water
Water hot
Watermelon
Wheat
Wheat bran
Wheat bulgur
Wheat flakes
Wheat flour
Wheat germ oil
Wheat semolina
Wheat semolina for children
White beans
White bread (wheat bread)
Zucchini

4.3 Use ingredients: little

Almond marzipan
Almond milk
Almond puree
Anchovy / Sardine
Anise (Common Fennel)
Apricot
Apricots
Bean oil
Beef bone marrow
Beef fillet
Beef heart
Beef kidney
Beef lungs (calf)
Beef meat
Beef meat (calf)
Beef meatbones
Beef stomach
Bitter melon
Black tea
Carrot
Carrot (Early Carrot)
Carrot juice without sugar
Chestnuts
Chicken meat
Clove
Coconut milk
Coriander
Corn
Corn (roasted)
Corn Grease (Polenta)
Cream, sweet 30%
Cumin (Caraway seed)
Curd cheese 20%
Curd cheese 40%
Dates dried
Deer meat
Deer meat
Dill
Eel
Eel smoked
Fennel
Fennel tea
French beans
Ginger fresh

Goose egg
Grass carp
Kefir
Kohlrabi
Marjoram
Multi-grain bread (gray bread)
Mustard seeds
Okra
Onion (shallot)
Onion (spring onion)
Onion read
Onion white
Oyster mushroom
Pepper Cayenne
Pepper white (ground)
Peppercorns
Peppers
Pheasant
Pineapple (from a can)
Pork heart
Pork knuckle
Pork meat
Pork skin
Pork stomach
Pumpkin
Pumpkin seed oil
Quail
Quail egg
Raisins
Sago (cereals)
Salt
Sour cream 15% fat
Sour milk
Sour milk cheese 20%
Soybean oil
Spiny lobsters
Star anise
Sugar brown
Sugar candy white
Sugar white
Turkey breast meat
Walnuts
Wheat beer

4.4 Do not use contra-acting foods

Basil (fresh)
Boxhorn clover seeds
Cereal coffee
Cherry

Cherry juice
Chicken egg
Chicken liver
Chicken yolk

Chili (pod or ground)
Chives
Chocolate
Cinnamon ground
Cinnamon sticks
Cocoa
Coffee
Curry
Feta cheese
Garlic
Ginger powder
Goat
Goat and sheep's milk
Goat cheese
Green spelt
Hawthorn
Hyssop
Juniper berry
Kumquats
Lamb bones
Lamb kidneys
Lamb liver
Lamb meat
Lamb shoulder
Leek
Lovage
Mold cheese
Mutton
Mutton
Nutmeg

Oat
Oat flakes (whole grain)
Oat flakes roasted
Oat flour
Oat fusion (baby food)
Oat meal
Oat milk
Oregano dried
Papaya
Parsley
Peaches
Peaches (canned)
Peppers (rose peppers)
Pimento
Pomegranate
Poppy
Radish (white, green, purple-red)
Red wine
Rose hip tea
Rosemary
Sake
Spirit
Sweet potato
Thyme
Turmeric (yellow root)
Umeboshi plums (Japanese apricots)
Vinegar (Apple vinegar)
White wine
Wild boar meat
Yogi tea

5 Complementary

5.1 Birch leaves

Folium Betulae
Preparation: Healing tea (infusion)
Emits moisture, cools moisture-heat in the bladder. Heat cooling in bi-syndromes with wind, moisture.
Pour 2 tablespoons of crushed birch leaves into 250 ml of boiling water, let stand for 10 minutes. Then sieve.
Drink one cup of it a day.

5.2 Chamomile

Chamaemelum nobile
Preparation: Healing tea (infusion)
Regulates liver-Qi, triggers stagnation, lowers liver-yang and internal
wind, regulates lung-qi, induces hot-mucus from the lungs, evokes wind-
heat and moisture-heat. Cooling.
Pour 2 teaspoons of the tea into 250 ml of boiling water and leave for 10
minutes. Then sieve. Drink 2 to 3 cups per day as needed.
Active ingredients: Äth. Oil: chamazulen, bisabolol, flavonoids, coumarins
Continuous use is not recommended, otherwise harmless.

5.3 Ginger fresh

Zingiberis officinalis, Rhizoma
Preparation: Decoction
Strengthens juices production, reduces cold-nuisance, stimulates,
stimulates the Yang-energy, warms the lung- and stomach-energy.
Put 1-6 slices of fresh root in a jug of water for 3 minutes. Drink 10 g in
two doses on empty stomach.
To improve the taste is brown raw sugar
Special features: In TCM, the fresh ginger root is mainly used against fish
poisoning and colds of the lungs and stomach. Because ginger promotes
nutrient uptake, it is often used in a variety of formulations to facilitate the
rapid absorption of other herbs and thereby enhance their effects. Ginger
contains the digestive enzyme zingibain. The digestive effect of this
substance is stronger than that of the enzyme papain.
In too large quantities, ginger leads to constipation, Not to use in:
pregnancy, high fever.

5.4 Lavender flowers

Lavandula angustifolia
Preparation: Healing tea (infusion)
Active ingredients: essential oil, tannins, flavonoids, phytosterols,
coumarins
Its aroma in the aroma lamp, as a bath additive or as a tea drunk, has a
relaxing effect on muscles and nerves. Helpful also for heart palpitations
and tension headache, internally against gastrointestinal complaints.

5.5 Peppermint

Menthae, Herba
Preparation: Healing tea (infusion)
Relieves the internal wind of the body, clears the head and eyes, detoxifies the skin. Moves and regulates qi, lowering stomach-qi. Clarifying wind-heat, detoxifying, moving.
Pour 2-10 g with 250 ml of boiling water and let stand for 10 minutes. Then sieve. Drink 2 to 3 cups per day as needed.
Active ingredients: essential oil (menthol), tannins, flavonoids, bitter substances
Do not cook for long; Do not use on: Biao-Xu sweating or pregnancy.

6 Basics of Nutrition

The basic principles of nutrition described herein are general recommendations. They are not aimed at a specific form of therapy. Recommendations concerning a therapy have priority.

6.1 Nutrition

Regular meals in a relaxed atmosphere. A warm breakfast is considered a good start into the day.

The main meals ought to be taken for lunch – supper in the early evening. Pay attention to feeling hungry or sated: don't eat too much nor remain hungry is the rule

Prepare the meals freshly from natural, regional products. Frozen, heat-conserved, industrially prepared or foodstuffs cooked in the microwave oven are rejected.

Choice of foodstuffs according to the season: more cooling food in summer, more warming food in winter.

Eat cooked food at least twice a day. Food and drinks ought to be lukewarm, never ice-cold or hot.

Raw vegetables, briefly cooked vegetables, freshly squeezed juices and mineral water are not recommended. Milk and dairy products are only included in the diet if they don't cause problems. Don't use therapeutic recipes over a longer period without consulting your doctor or therapist.

Varied food
Enjoy the diversity of foodstuffs. Characteristics of a balanced nutrition are variety, suitable combination and a balanced quantity of rich and low energy foodstuffs (on one hand avoiding undersupply with essential nutrients and on the other hand to take to many undesirable substances).

A lot of Cereal Products - and Potatoes
Bread, pasta, rice, cereal flakes (best wholemeal) as well as potatoes contain almost no fat, but many vitamins, mineral nutrients, trace elements, roughage and secondary plant substances. These foodstuffs ought to be taken with low-fat side dishes.

Vegetables and Fruit – „Take Five" every day ... 5 portions of vegetables and fruit a day, as fresh as possible, briefly cooked, or maybe one portion as a juice – ideal as a side dish to every meal as well as snack between meals: Thus a lot of vitamins, mineral nutrients as well as roughage and secondary plant substances

Daily milk and dairy products

Milk and Dairy Products every Day, once or twice per Week Fish; meat, sausages as well as eggs moderately. These foodstuffs contain valuable nutrients like calcium in the milk, iodine selenium and omega-3 fat acids in saltwater fish. Meat is favorable due to its high content of disposable iron and the vitamins B1, B6 and B12. Quantities of 300 – 600 g meat and sausage per week are sufficient. Prefer low-fat products, especially in meat- and dairy products.

Low-fat and fatty Foodstuffs

Fat supplies us with essential fat acids and fatty foodstuffs contain also fat-soluble vitamins. Fat is high in energy; therefore much fat in the food may cause overweight, possibly also cancer. Too many saturated fat acids may further a tendency for cardio-vascular diseases in the long term. Prefer vegetable oils and fats (e.g. rapeseed-, olive-, soya-oils and solid fats produced therefrom). Beware of invisible fat in meat- and dairy products, pastry and sweets as well as in fast-food and convenience foods. 70 – 90 g fat per day is sufficient.

Moderately Sugar and Salt

Take sugar and foods/drinks containing various kinds of sugar (e.g. glucose syrup) only occasionally. Use herbs and spices as well as a little salt creatively. Prefer salt containing iodine.

Plenty of Liquids

Water is absolutely essential. Drink 1-2 l liquids every day. Prefer water (with or without gas) and other low-calorie drinks. Alcoholic drinks should not be taken.

Tasty Dishes, carefully cooked

Cook the meals with as low temperatures and as short as possible, using little water and fat – this preserves the original taste, keeps the nutrients intact and prevents the production of harmful compounds.

Take time and enjoy the food

Take your Time and enjoy your Food
Eating consciously helps to eat right. The eye enjoys food, too. It's fun, invites to enjoy varied dishes and stimulates the feeling of satiety.

Watch your Weight and stay in Motion

A balanced diet and a lot of exercise and sport (30 – 60 min/day) are a healthy combination. The right weight furthers well-being and health.

Thermals, directional effectiveness, digestive power
There are various criteria for judging the effectiveness of herbs and foodstuffs.
The use of certain herbs and ingredients is based on observations of the effects on the body which these foodstuffs, herbs and spices show after having eaten them. The medical science has developed following system: Every ingredient or herb has a directional effectiveness. Furthermore, there are herbs which have a special effect on certain organs.
The basic condition for a healthy metabolism is to obtain sufficient energy from food and that the digestive process doesn't use too much energy. An easily digestible meal makes content and sated, doesn't cause flatulence and fatigue after the meal. The perfect spices increase the healthiness of our meals. Very often, just small doses of herbs and spices will suffice. They are not used to make us sated, but to help our digestive organs to digest the food.

6.2   Recipes

The recipes list the ingredients to be used and the cooking instructions show how the dish is prepared. The list of ingredients shows the concerned quantities as well as the relevance for the therapy. If you find „omit", try to comply or find an alternative from the „list of recommended foodstuffs". Mostly it shall result just in a small change of taste when you simply avoid this ingredient.
Mild cooking methods: boiling, stewing, poaching, steaming
Strong cooking methods: barbecuing, roasting, frying, smoking
Balanced cooking methods: deep-frying, baking brick
Deep-freezing and warming in the microwave oven should be avoided (denaturalization).

6.3   Foodstuffs

Foodstuffs have an effect on body and soul like medicinal herbs, only a very much milder one. Dietary advice is mainly based on regional foodstuffs. The knowledge about the effects of each foodstuff and the knowledge, when which foodstuff shall be used, is based on the school medicine. Use ecologic-organic products, if possible. As everything should be cooked for a long time due to a better digestability and very rarely eaten raw, the food agrees with everyone.
The classification of the foodstuffs according to their effect on the body is the basis in order to achieve a harmonious status of health.
Dietary advisors do not recommend certain foodstuffs for everyone. The individual diet is tailor-made for the individual constitution.

Buy only fresh and ripe fruit and vegetables. You ought to leave unripe fruit and vegetables and such with brown spots and wilted leaves behind in the market. In this case take deep-frozen goods (never ready-to-serve dishes!). Fruit and vegetables are deep-frozen immediately after harvesting and often contain more vitamins and minerals than the goods from the vegetable shelf. Whereas conserved or tinned goods contain very much less biological substances. Also, salt, sugar and others are mostly added to the latter. Never leave the foodstuffs in the water after washing them to avoid that many vital substances get drowned. Clean salads, fruit and vegetables immediately before serving.

Please make sure of the hygienic processing of foodstuffs. Clean your salads, fruit and vegetables carefully. When cooking with meat, prepare all ingredients first and then process the meat products. Clean the worktop and tools very carefully. Wooden surfaces ought to be treated with a mild disinfectant regularly in order to reduce germination.
Store fruit and vegetables separately, if possible. Harvested fruit and vegetables are still alive and emit e.g. ethylene gas, which makes other products ripen and age faster. Keep meat and fish in the closed packaging or store them in the fridge in closed containers.

6.4 Herbs

There are some basic rules for storing medicinal herbs. On principle, herbs must be protected from direct sunlight, humidity and heat.

Containers for the storage of herbs may be glasses, ceramic jars and even plastic containers. However, plastic is a rather unsuitable material and should only be a short-term solution. In case of glass containers, use a dark material.

Medicinal herbs cannot be kept for any long period. The shelf life of herbs is limited. However, it can be prolonged with suitable storage. The place should be dark, rather cool and absolutely dry. A wooden medicine cabinet, placed not directly next to a source of heat, would be ideal. Never buy large quantities of herbs so as not to have to throw them away. Label the container with the name of the herb and the date of harvesting or processing.

7 Other dietic-books

The following syndromes of dietetics, TCM or for a therapy supplement for cancer are available.

Dietetics

E001. Nutrition of the infant - baby food
E002. Nutrition during lactation
E003. Nutrition in old age
E004. Nutrition of children and adolescents
E005. Nutrition of athletes
E006. Light weight
E007. Pregnancy
E008. Full food

Protein and electrolyte - kidneys
E009. (hemodialysis) dialysis treatment
E010. Acute renal failure
E011. Chronic renal insufficiency
E012. Nephrotic syndrome
E013. Kidney stones (nephrolithiasis)

Gastrointestinal tract - pancreas
E014. Acute pancreatitis (inflammation of the pancreas)
E015. Chronic pancreatitis (inflammation of the pancreas)

Gastrointestinal tract - small intestine and large intestine
E016. Acute obstipation (constipation)
E017. Chronic obstipation (constipation)
E018. Colon irritabile
E019. Diverticulitis
E020. Acquired lactose intolerance (lactose malabsorption)
E021. Fructose malabsorption
E022. Glutensensitive enteropathy (celiac disease)
E023. Colectomy
E024. Short Bowel Syndrome

Gastrointestinal tract - liver, gallbladder, bile ducts
E025. Acute and chronic hepatitis (inflammation of the liver)
E026. Cholelithiasis (bile stones)
E027. fatty liver
E028. cirrhosis

Gastrointestinal tract - Stomach and duodenal intestine
E029. Acute gastritis
E030. Chronic gastritis

E031. Stomach bleeding
E032. Ulcus ventriculi and duodenal ulcer
E033. Condition after gastric surgery

Gastrointestinal tract - oral cavity and esophagus
E034. Stomatitis
E035. Esophageal carcinoma (esophageal cancer)
E036. Refluosophagitis (heartburn)

Special diseases
E037. Phenylketonuria (PKU)
E038. Rheumatic joint diseases

Metabolism
E039. Obesity (overweight)
E040. Diabetes mellitus
E041. Eating disorders (underweight)

Fat metabolism
E042. Hypercholesterolaemia (increased cholesterol level)
E043. Hepatic Encephalopathy

Heart and circulation
E044. Arteriosclerosis (arterial calcification)
E045. Heart insufficiency
E046. Hypertension
E047. Hyperuricaemia and gout

Changed nutrient requirements
E048. In case of fever
E049. For malignant diseases
E050. After burns
E051. Radiation and chemotherapy

CANCER
E100. Pancreatic cancer
E101. Bladder cancer
E102. Blood cancer (leukemia)
E103. Breast cancer
E104. Colorectal cancer
E105. Gastric cancer
E106. Kidney cancer
E107. Esophageal cancer

TCM
E200. Bladder - moisture heat in the bladder
E201. Bladder - moisture and cold in the bladder
E202. Bladder - emptiness and cold in the bladder
E203. Large intestine - external cold affects the large intestine
E204. Large intestine - moisture heat in the large intestine
E205. Large intestine - heat blocks the intestine II acute
E206. Large intestine - dryness of the colon

E207. Large intestine - Yang deficiency (cold)
E208. Heart - Blood insufficiency
E209. Heart - Blood stagnation
E210. Heart - Fire
E211. Heart - Hot mucus clogs the heart pores
E212. Heart - Cold mucus clogs the heart pores
E213. Heart - Qi deficiency
E214. Heart - Yang deficiency
E215. Heart - Yin deficiency
E216. Liver - Ascending Liver Yang
E217. Liver - Blood deficiency
E218. Liver - Blood stagnation
E219. Liver - Moisture heat in liver and gall bladder
E220. Liver - Fire
E221. Liver - Gall bladder Qi-Empty
E222. Liver - Cold in the liver meridian
E223. Liver - Qi stagnation
E224. Liver - Wind
E225. Liver - Wind with ascending liver Yang
E226. Liver - Wind with blood anemic
E227. Liver - Wind with extreme heat
E228. Lung - Qi deficiency
E229. Lung - Mucus-moisture in the lungs
E230. Lung - Mucus-heat in the lungs
E231. Lung - Mucus-cold in the lungs
E232. Lung - Dryness of the lungs
E233. Lung - Wind-heat attacks the lungs
E234. Lung - Wind-cold affects the lungs
E235. Lung - Yin deficiency
E236. Stomach - Bloodstagnation
E237. Stomach - Fire
E238. Stomach - Cold with liquid
E239. Stomach - Nutrition stagnation
E240. Stomach - Qi deficiency
E241. Stomach - Rebellious Qi
E242. Stomach - Yin Emptiness
E243. Spleen - Heat and moisture attack the spleen
E244. Spleen - Coldness and moisture affects the spleen
E245. Spleen - Qi deficiency
E246. Spleen - Qi deficiency + Declining spleen Qi
E247. Spleen - Qi deficiency + spleen does not control the blood
E248. Spleen - Yang deficiency
E249. Kidney - Heart and kidney no longer communicate
E250. Kidney - Jing deficiency
E251. Kidney - Kidneys cannot receive the Qi
E252. Kidney - Qi is not stable
E253. Kidney - Yang deficiency
E254. Kidney - Yin deficiency

For further information visit nutribook.info.

8 EBNS - Software for nutritional counseling

The main task of the database is to create personalized nutritional advice for each patient individually. The database was developed for Dietetics and Traditional Chinese Medicine.
The Database supports training and advices in the daily work routine.

The computer program provides lists of recipes, ingredients and herbs, which are given to the client. individually adjustable according to patient's request from whole food to vegetarians (lacto, ovo, ...). For every register there is an information sheet which can be given to the client. All texts can be individually designed.

The syndromes can be combined and result in an intersection of the recommended recipes and ingredients. The automated diagnosis for the TCM enables you to check your experience during the training as well as to confirm your diagnosis in the working day. You select several predefined symptoms and have the program automatically display the relevant syndromes.

How to work with the database:
Select the patient / client, select one or more of the syndromes you diagnosed and print the folder.

You can change all values, create new symptoms or syndromes, develop recipes, change or adapt ingredients and herbs to your findings. In simple client management, all relevant data about the person is stored. You get an overview of the past diagnoses and the development of the course of the disease.

As a consultant you save a lot of time when you print out the recipe, food and herbal lists for the recognized syndromes and give them to the clients. You can use this time for a personal conversation. With the database, dieticians and nutritionists can view the nutrients and trace elements for each recipe and develop recipes for syndromes even with suggested ingredients.

All recipe and grocery lists can also be ordered from me as a combination of several diseases. I wish all readers good luck, health and happiness in life.
More information can be found at www.ebns.at.

Volunteer: www.krebsinfo.at
Josef Miligui